ISAAC THOMAS HECKER

Isaac Thomas Hicks
bronze
Fred Smith

ISAAC THOMAS HECKER

Spiritual Pilgrim

JOHN J. BEHNKE, CSP

Paulist Press
New York / Mahwah, NJ

#9539|8512

Photo/Image Credits: See page xi.
Cover images: Background photo by Everett Historical / Shutterstock.com. Fr. Hecker image courtesy of the Paulist Archives.
Cover design by Sharyn Banks
Book design by Lynn Else

Library of Congress Cataloging-in-Publication Data

Names: Behnke, John, author.
Title: Isaac Thomas Hecker : spiritual pilgrim / John J. Behnke, CSP.
Description: New York : Paulist Press, 2017. | Includes bibliographical references.
Identifiers: LCCN 2016026444 (print) | LCCN 2016034012 (ebook) | ISBN 9780809149537 (pbk. : alk. paper) | ISBN 9781587685521 (Ebook)
Subjects: LCSH: Hecker, Isaac Thomas, 1819-1888. | Paulist Fathers—United States—Biography. | Catholic converts—United States—Biography. | Catholic Church—United States—History—19th century.
Classification: LCC BX4705.H4 B45 2017 (print) | LCC BX4705.H4 (ebook) | DDC 271/.79 [B] —dc23
LC record available at https://lccn.loc.gov/2016026444

ISBN 978-0-8091-4953-7 (paperback)
ISBN 978-1-58768-552-1 (e-book)

Published by Paulist Press
997 Macarthur Boulevard
Mahwah, New Jersey 07430

www.paulistpress.com

Printed and bound in the
United States of America

CONTENTS

PREFACE

Isaac Thomas Hecker: A Man for Our Times

I grew up in a family in which some of my relatives were German Lutherans and some were German Catholics. My father's side was Lutheran. The Catholics in the family didn't know too much about the Lutheran religious practices; in the 1940s and 1950s we weren't allowed to attend any Protestant services. It was forbidden by the common Catholic teaching of the time. When someone from my father's side of the family got married, we'd arrive at the church late and not go inside for the ceremony. Instead, we'd wait and throw rice as the newlyweds came out of the church. After all the relatives came out, I'd sheepishly climb the steps of the church and peer through the front doors to see if I could figure out what might have been going on in there that was so forbidden to us Catholics. Then my immediate family members would proceed to the reception hall with the rest of the guests.

By the 1960s the rules of the Catholic Church had undergone some change. I entered the seminary in 1962. Our history professor would arrange for us to have a tour of a number of Protestant churches. We would not only study church architecture, but also began to learn something of the differing views held by these denominations.

Life seemed pretty simple in the 1950s. We believed that the United States was the greatest country in the world, one that provided liberty and freedom for all. We were convinced that our church had the unchanging truth and that if we kept the rules, the rules would keep us. The world changed drastically between the 1950s and the 1960s.

We came to realize that our country did not offer liberty and freedom equally to all its citizens. There was a lot of social unrest. The civil rights movement was just getting underway. The world was not safe and secure, either; we came to realize that World War II did not bring final and lasting peace to all places and to all countries. The church didn't seem to have all the immediate answers to life as we once thought it had.

It was a time of searching, looking, and seeking.

In the history classes I took in seminary, I began to learn that upheaval and uncertainty were not new to the world scene, even though I was experiencing it for the first time. Every few generations seemed to live through a major change in society.

In this time of personal awakening for me, we were studying about the life and times of Isaac Thomas Hecker, the founder of the Paulist Fathers. His society was fresh with idealism harvested from the victory of the American Revolution, which freed the former English colonies from foreign rule. But it was also experiencing the exploitation of countless workers who were then chained to the wheels and cogs of the Industrial Revolution that was sweeping the continent. The country was expanding to the western coastland of California, and this vast new expanse opened the challenge of new opportunities to those who were searching for adventure and meaning in their lives.

Isaac Hecker, called the "earnest seeker" by some who knew him, was born in this changing time. He looked for answers, for meaning in his life, and for solutions to the problems of the society in which he lived. In the idealism of his teenage years, he joined a breakaway political party. He attended different denominational services in search of the "right" religion, joined a few utopian alternative-living communes that were looking for a way of life that spoke to him about being of service to others, and finally, when he concluded that Catholicism offered the proper direction for his life, he joined the Catholic Church. Then, when he realized that his life's calling was to serve God in ministerial work, he became a member of the Congregation of the Most Holy Redeemer, or Redemptorist Fathers.

Isaac Hecker had the boldness and the courage to start his own religious community when he saw an opportunity to serve God in new ways that spoke of the ideals that the people in the United States had come to claim as their own through the writings of the Declaration of Independence and the Constitution of the United States. New avenues were opened to him and to his followers.

I was mesmerized by Isaac's life, his insights, and his idealism. I was captivated by his integrity, by his searching, by his way of opening doors of opportunity and walking through them, by his searching and seeking and wonderment. In many ways, Isaac's longing, searching, seeking, and finding meaning in his life paralleled my own. Isaac's searching was my searching. Isaac's seeking is the seeking that we all must do. His faithfully living out of the answers he found is still a model for us to follow. Isaac Thomas Hecker is a man for our times.

IMAGE CREDITS

Fr. Frank Sabatté, CSP, http://www.sabatteart.com/: the sculpture of Fr. Hecker in the frontispiece and the sculpture of the Four Paulist Founders in chapter 7.

Wikimedia Commons: the portrait of Orestes Brownson in chapter 3; the photograph of Fruitlands in chapter 4; and the picture of the Wittem Convent in chapter 6.

The Paulist Archives: the cover photograph of Isaac Hecker; photographs of Frs. Augustine Hewit and George Deshon in chapter 6; the picture of Cardinal Barnabò in chapter 6; the photograph of the original Paulist residence in chapter 7; the picture of George Hecker in chapter 7; and the photograph of Isaac Hecker in the 1880s in chapter 8.

Nancy de Flon private collection: the Croton Flour Mills trade card in chapter 2 and the photograph of John Henry Newman in chapter 5.

Nancy de Flon Photography: the photographs of the detail of Fr. Hecker's tomb in chapter 8 and the baptismal font at St. Paul the Apostle Church in chapter 9.

CHRONOLOGY OF ISAAC HECKER'S LIFE

1819
Born December 18

1830
Works in his brothers' bakery

1834
Meets Orestes A. Brownson

1843
January–July: Brook Farm
July 11–25: Fruitlands
August: Returns to New York

1844
April–June: Studies in Concord
August 1: Baptized

1845
Meets Redemptorist Fathers
July: Sails for Belgium
August 31: Begins Redemptorist novitiate

1846
October 15: Redemptorist profession
October 16: Goes to Wittem to study

1848

September: Sent to London to serve at St. Mary's, Clapham

1849

October 23: Ordained priest in London by Bishop
Nicholas Wiseman

1850

Begins parish mission career in Liverpool, England

1851

March 19: Returns to New York

1852–1857

Life as Redemptorist in America
1855: Publishes *Questions of the Soul*
1857: Publishes *Aspirations of Nature*
August 26: Arrives in Rome to discuss plan for founding
an English-speaking Redemptorist house
August 29: Dismissed from Redemptorist Community
December 22: First audience with Pope Pius IX

1858

March 6: Decree of the Congregation of Bishops and
Regulars releasing Hecker and the four Fathers
from the Redemptorist Order
May: Returns to New York
July 7: Paulist Rules approved by Archbishop Hughes
of New York

1859

June 19: The corner stone at 59th St. is laid
November 24: The house is completed

1865

April: Founding of *The Catholic World*

1866

Founding of The Catholic Publication Society
(Paulist Press)

1869

November 26: Arrives in Rome for the Vatican Council

1870

June: Returns to New York
Founding of *The Young Catholic*

1871

Health deteriorates due to chronic leukemia

1872

Travels to Florida for his health

1873–1875

Travels abroad to Europe and Egypt

1875

October: Returns to New York

1887

February: Publishes *The Church and the Age*

1888

February 14: Death of his brother George
December 22: Isaac Thomas Hecker dies at the
Paulist House in Manhattan

1

INTRODUCTION

Some stories just need to be told. They seem to capture a segment of life in an interesting way. They depict an exciting way in which a person or persons have chosen to live out their lives. Some stories are just easy to relate to.

Isaac Hecker's life was one such story. When Isaac was born in the early 1800s, the United States was only a few decades old. His life captured the enthusiasm for adventure and for living life to the fullest that pervaded the newly formed country.

Isaac was born in New York City of German immigrant parents. He searched for meaning in his life through a number of different avenues that were available to him. As a teenager he threw himself into the idealism of a fledgling political party that tried to make a difference in the way people were treated, especially the worker and the downtrodden. When he didn't find its solutions to be satisfactory, he searched for other ways to give meaning to his life and to influence those around him for the better.

One of these ways was to participate in different utopian alternative-lifestyle communities. These communities, whose members called themselves Transcendentalists, sought the beauty of nature and being of mutual help to one another. Using their natural abilities to draw upon their inner spirituality, they were able to experience the presence of God in their lives. Isaac also looked into many different religious traditions and denominations, including

Methodism, Episcopalianism, Calvinism (the Reformed tradition), Unitarianism, (Christian) Universalism, and the Mormons,[1] before finding the Catholic Church and becoming an ordained priest.

Isaac was a true American and believed in the principles upon which the United States was founded. The union of the states into one country gave a sense of stability in the new republic in which he was born. The equally important idea of being free to think and do what one was capable of thinking and doing also played a major role in helping him to formulate his dreams of a Catholic America. He liked the idea of belonging to a Church that had its foundation at the time of Jesus. That such a church had a set of dogmas that helped coalesce people into a united group of believers appealed to him, as did the idea that the Holy Spirit was involved in shaping people anew for the age in which they were living. "Old truths in new forms" was an idea that he saw manifest in his own time.

Isaac had big dreams of creating a Catholic America and, eventually, reclaiming Europe for Catholicism. He encouraged others to help him make the dream a reality. People clamored to hear him preach and stood in line to listen to his lectures. They wanted to read what he was writing. He started a religious community people wanted to join.

And so Isaac Thomas Hecker's life begins.

---

1. *Methodism* is a group of Protestant denominations inspired by the teachings of John Wesley (1703–91). With its emphasis on social service, Methodism has historically attracted adherents from all sectors of society. Much of the great treasury of Christian hymnody derives from eminent Methodists, especially from John Wesley's brother, Charles. When King Henry VIII of England (1491–1547) was refused a divorce from his wife Catherine of Aragon, Henry formally rejected the authority of the Pope. The resulting Church of England, or Anglican Church, is called *Episcopalian* in the United States. Classical *Calvinists* believe in the depravity of human nature and the absolute sovereignty of God, who predestines people to heaven or hell. *Unitarians* belong to a Christian denomination that holds that God is one entity, in contrast to Christians who believe in a three-personed God (the Trinity). *Universalism* (or Christian Universalism) believes in the doctrine of universal reconciliation: all people will eventually be reconciled to God. The members of the Church of Jesus Christ of Latter-day Saints, founded by Joseph Smith in the early 1830s, are called *Mormons*. In addition to the Bible, the Book of Mormon is their sacred book.

2

THE YOUNG ISAAC HECKER

Born of Protestant parents and in the midst of a
Protestant community, no positive religious instructions
were imparted to me in my youth, and my religious
belief, therefore, was left for me to decide…at some
future period and according to my own choice. At the
early age of twelve years, my mind began to seek after
the truth and my heart was moved with the desire of
doing to others.

—Document submitted by Fr. Hecker to his
director and others, Rome, 1858

Most young boys love taking things apart to see how they are
made, especially mechanical things such as a watch. Isaac Thomas
Hecker, as a young boy, liked putting things together. His maternal
grandfather was a clock maker with whom he spent a good deal of
time in his clock shop. With the help of his grandfather, Isaac made
a wall clock. For years it hung in the Methodist Church he attended
with his mother in their neighborhood in lower Manhattan.

Born in New York City on December 18, 1819, Isaac was an
inquisitive boy who enjoyed sitting out on the docks of the East

River at night, gazing at the stars and contemplating eternal mysteries far beyond his ability to comprehend.

Isaac's immediate family consisted of his maternal grandfather, Engel Friend (Freund); his father, John; his mother, Caroline; two brothers, John and George; and a sister, Elizabeth. (Another brother died in infancy.)

At one time Isaac's father owned a foundry and had helped build the boiler for the first commercially successful steamboat, designed by Robert Fulton and named the *Clermont*. His mother was a religious person who attended church regularly. She instilled in her children a sense of reverence and awe for God and taught them their prayers.

The Hecker family lived unscathed through the yellow fever epidemic that ravaged lower Manhattan in 1822. Not long after, however, Isaac contracted smallpox, which nearly killed him. He was so sick that his mother explained to him that he was probably going to die. Isaac assured her that he wasn't going to die, because he felt that God had some important work for him to do when he got older. As a young boy he probably didn't realize how true his "prediction" would become. He did recover, but the disease left his face permanently pockmarked.

When Isaac reached the age of seven, his parents thought that he should be in school, and so they enrolled him in Public School #7, on Chrystie Street, near his home. As was the practice, Isaac learned his ABCs by tracing the letters in a tray of sand using a stick about the size of a pencil to form the letters. When the tray was filled with the practice letters, a strip of leather was used to erase them from the sand so that he could practice some more. He also learned how to read and to add and subtract, and studied the Bible.

But hard times fell on the family. Business at their father's foundry started to decline. The older boys, John and George, teenagers by now, went to work at an uncle's bakery on Hester Street. Isaac, just twelve, was taken out of school and found a job at a Methodist-owned publishing house, the *Christian Advocate and Journal*. He folded papers, preparing them to be mailed. Since this position did not pay enough, he left and started working in a type-print foundry. Eventually he joined his two older brothers in the bakery business.

When John turned twenty-one, he and George started their own bakery business and brought Isaac with them. Isaac started as an errand boy. He learned to watch the ovens and eventually was taught how to mix dough and bake cakes. Isaac would deliver the baked goods in a cart he pushed along the streets. Sometimes, in the snow, Isaac's cart would get stuck in the mud and he would be unable to get it loose himself. He had to rely on a passersby to help him get his cart, full of bakery goods, moving again. Twelve-hour days left the brothers exhausted.

CROTON FLOUR MILLS TRADE CARD

This nineteenth-century version of a business card shows the Croton Flour Mills owned and run by the Hecker brothers. The business was located in Manhattan, under where the Manhattan Bridge is now.

Over the years, the Hecker Brothers owned a number of bakeries and ground their own flour at a mill they named Croton Flour Mills. A contemporary publication had this to say about Croton Flour Mills:

> Geo. V. Hecker & Co. Croton Flour Mills. Office No. 205 Cherry Street [Manhattan].—A representative and old-established house in the metropolis, extensively engaged in the manufacture of flour and the like, is that of Messrs. Geo. V. Hecker & Co., whose Croton Flour Mills are centrally located in Cherry Street. This business was established in 1843 by Geo. V. Hecker & Bro., and was conducted by them till 1874, when the present firm succeeded to the management.[1]

It goes on to say that the Mills "are among the largest and most complete in the United States." The Hecker brothers' prosperity would go on to play an important role in Isaac's later ventures.

---

1. *Illustrated New York: The Metropolis of Today* (1888), p. 188.

A NEW DIRECTION

Why should not those who profess Christianity imitate Christ in devoting themselves entirely to the spreading of the truth, the relief of the poor, and the elevation of the lower classes? Such like thoughts occupied my mind, and since a social reform was needed, it was my duty to begin with myself, and this led me to treat those in my employ with greater kindness, and to make important changes in my way of living.

—Document submitted by Fr. Hecker to his
director and others, Rome, 1858

As businessmen in charge of a large number of employees, the three Hecker brothers were especially troubled by the exploitation of laborers in New York City. It was a time when the industrialists, who had most of the money, paid their employees deplorably scant wages and treated their employees more as commodities than as human beings. Isaac's brothers believed that involvement in politics was the way to solve many of the social problems of their day. They joined the Equal Rights Party, which was started in the 1830s as an offshoot of the Democratic Party in New York City. Members of the Equal Rights Party opposed the big monopolies of the time as well as all special interest groups. They were called Loco-Focos because they had a "local focus" on how politics and government should be involved in people's lives. The platform of the party included, among other things, that the government should protect the rights of all. Special rights for special groups were rejected and special interest groups were to be avoided. Government was to be only as big as was needed to assure the equal rights of all; it was not to become a national monopoly.

When not working at the bakery, Isaac could be found handing out leaflets. Around election time, although he was not old enough to vote, he could be seen standing on a soapbox making speeches in favor of the platform his party was espousing. Isaac and his brothers believed that the way to better peoples' living and working conditions was through political reform of society. Isaac poured his heart and soul into this endeavor, until, one day, he became totally disenchanted by the bickering and by the fighting and corruption he saw in politicians and in the political parties of his time.

Although Isaac lost interest in reform through politics, he never lost interest in social reform. Orville Dewey, a Unitarian minister who came to New York in 1835—and four years later dedicated a new church, the Church of the Messiah, near the Heckers' home—caught Isaac's attention. He started attending the church services on Sundays and was captivated by the eloquence of Dewey's sermons supporting the rights of the laborer and the need for human welfare of all people. Isaac started reading all the books he could find on religion and philosophy.

Dewey's emphasis on "practical religion," which he defined as "a religion that has the most intimate connection with our daily life and welfare,"[1] appealed to Isaac's own inclinations, and Isaac began to suspect that he might have a vocation. He wasn't sure what a

---

1. Orville Dewey, *A Discourse Delivered at the Dedication of the Church of the Messiah* (New York: Stationer's Hall, 1839), 11–12.

vocation would entail, but he felt that the ordinary means of working in the business world was not what he should be doing with his life. He knew he could think on his feet and that he was a fairly good orator, with all the practice he had trying to coax people to accept and vote his party line views. But what he should be doing with his life, he really didn't know.

Living in New York, Isaac had many opportunities to hear good speakers on almost any topic imaginable. About the time he became disillusioned with politics, another person came into Isaac's life as he traversed along the path searching for answers and truth. This person was Orestes Brownson.

ORESTES BROWNSON

Orestes Brownson, like Isaac Hecker, was a spiritual seeker who himself became Catholic. This impelled Hecker to consider Catholicism seriously, much as John Henry Newman's turn to Rome brought many other conversions to Catholicism in its wake.

Brownson himself had been an avid seeker in his own life. He had even formed his own church for a while in Boston. Brownson helped shape Hecker's idea that American politics and religion could work together for the welfare of humanity. He wanted to see the kingdom of God for all here and now. If Orestes Brownson, a native of Boston, spoke in New York, Isaac and his brothers would attend the lecture. They liked his talks so much that he was often a guest in their home. The theme of his talks usually combined two things close to Isaac's heart: democracy and Christianity. Brownson was about fifteen years older than Isaac and, over the course of time, Isaac began to look up to him as a mentor. They became longtime friends. Little did Isaac know, at that early stage, what an important influence Orestes Brownson was to be in his life.

4

THE SPIRITUAL SEEKER

Oh heavenly Father wilt thou give me heavenly grace
and strength to keep getting better to over come all
temptations that may beset my path. Oh Lord awaken
me more to the divine capacities thou hast endowed
Man with and willt thou make my sight clearer and my
hearing delicater that I may see more and more of thy
law and hear more and more of thy divine voice of love.

—*Diary*, August 9, 1843

For a number of years, Isaac Hecker committed his thoughts to a diary. He was an extraordinarily prolific writer; between 1843 and 1845 alone, he filled five notebooks with reflections on how he could improve himself, what he should be doing with his life, and the dreams he had for the future. He also composed beautiful, almost poetic prayers directed to God. When Isaac was not sure what he wanted to do with his life, he would question himself, trying to discover answers through his writing.

A prayerful and pensive person, he often spent a long time in his room alone, pondering, praying, and journaling. For a young man he was extremely spiritual and found great comfort in his prayer life.

At some time during the summer of 1842, Isaac, then twenty-two years old, had a mystical experience, the details of which he confided to his journal in May 1843:

> I saw…a beautiful angelic, pure being and myself standing alongside of her, feeling a most heavenly pure joy. And it was as if our bodies were luminous and they gave forth a moonlike light, which I felt sprang from the joy that we experienced. We were unclothed, pure and unconscious of anything but pure love and joy, and I felt as if we had always lived together and that our motions, actions, feelings and thoughts came from one center…. Now this vision continually hovers over me….I am charmed by its influence, and I am conscious that, if I should accept anything else, I should lose the life which would be the only existence wherein I could say I live.[1]

The effect of this powerful vision and other mystical experiences was that Isaac lost all interest in the business in which he was involved with his brothers and came also to believe that he was not meant to marry and raise a family. George and John were perplexed; their flour business now had not only its own flour mill, the Croton Flour Mill in Lower Manhattan, but also a chain of six bakeries, and their youngest brother was not pulling his weight. What to do?

Meanwhile, Isaac himself began to realize that to follow the path on which this angelic being was leading him was not going to be easy; in fact, it would be a path of suffering. Consequently, he was plunged into depression and doubt. He decided to visit Orestes Brownson in Massachusetts and, while there, wrote his brothers a

---

1. Quoted in Robert W. Baer, CSP, "A Jungian Analysis of Isaac Thomas Hecker," in *Hecker Studies: Essays on the Thought of Isaac Hecker*, ed. John Farina (New York: Paulist Press, 1983), 138.

letter in which he expressed his doubts and fears: "How this will end I know not, but can not but trust God. It is not my will but my destiny, which will not be one of ease and pleasure."[2]

Brownson suggested to Isaac that he consider joining Brook Farm, a Transcendentalist community near Boston. It was an experimental living community of intelligent people of all types, from scholars and artists to farmers and tradesmen—Transcendentalists, searching together for the meaning of life. Transcendentalism held that the ideal spiritual state goes beyond the physical and empirical, and that a person reaches that state by personal intuition rather than religious doctrine. Transcendentalists also preferred natural settings as a way of coming to an understanding of one's inner spirituality.

The idea appealed to the young Hecker. He, too, was searching for the truth. This might be exactly what he was looking for. He could hone his ideas of social reform and deepen his spiritual longings with a group of intellectuals steeped in the ideals of Transcendentalism.

In January 1843, twenty-three-year-old Isaac went to Brook Farm to embark on his search for truth. Most of the people there not only paid some money for room and board, but also did some kind of manual labor to supplement their upkeep. Isaac became their baker. Everyone was more than pleased with the quality of the bread he baked daily.

Many of the people residing there—including such eminent minds as Thoreau, Nathaniel Hawthorne, and Emerson—taught courses to those who were interested. Isaac took classes in French, music, and philosophy. It was here that he came under the influence of Unitarian minister Dr. William Ellery Channing. Channing

---

2. Ibid., 141.

believed—and this struck a chord with young Hecker—that people possessed the inner power to improve themselves. By discovering their inner self, they could find common norms of living that everyone could agree upon: civility, human responsibility, character, virtues, restraint, a call to serve the common good. Through searching within oneself one could find a spiritual path, common to all, to truth: a oneness with self and nature, and self and others.

On weekends, the inhabitants (some seventy) went to different denominational churches for services. Isaac usually attended the services Brownson held nearby. He was interested in the influence that institutional religion had in bringing about the betterment of humanity, although no specific church held any particular attraction for him.

It was at Brook Farm that he realized that he was becoming a mystic. He had a real sense of the presence of God in his life. He experienced the presence of God in the beauty of nature, in his journaling and writing, and in his quiet, prayerful moments. He relished these moments of peace and serenity and longed for more of them. Yet he knew he had to do some sort of meaningful work that would bring him a salary on which to live. He loved the spiritual and contemplative, but he also knew he had to have a livelihood. It was a real struggle for him as he tried to find balance and meaning in his life.

By this time his brother John had joined the Episcopalian Church. During Isaac's visit home in the spring of 1843, John tried to get Isaac to attend a service with him. Isaac, not so inclined at that point, suggested that he would wait until all the churches were joined together as one.

Meanwhile, however, he investigated Episcopalianism by reading a copy of the *Tracts for the Times* that his brothers had given him. The *Tracts* were written by members of the Oxford Movement, a group of dons from Oxford University who wanted to demonstrate the apostolic origins of the Anglican Church, or Church of England, and thus prove its legitimacy as a rightful part of the church instituted by Christ; in other words, it was "the Catholic Church on English soil." John Henry Newman (1801–90) was its most prominent member until he converted to Roman Catholicism in 1845.

On Easter Sunday, Isaac went to the Catholic Church for services. He was very caught up with the beauty of the church and the symbolism he found throughout the building. While praying during the service, he felt a genuine presence of God there. He was impressed with the beautiful music, the prayerfulness of the people, and the pageantry of the ceremony he witnessed.

FRUITLANDS

During his stay at Fruitlands, a community in Harvard, Massachusetts, run by Bronson Alcott, Hecker came to realize that institutional religion, rather than elitist small communities, would provide the means of bringing about social reform.

Although he learned a great deal about life at Brook Farm and made many close friends there, Isaac was beginning to suspect that it did not hold the answer for him, as he made no progress toward confirming the validity of what seemed to be his mystical experiences. "I want God's living work to do," he wrote in his diary. He decided instead to try another Harvard-based community called Fruitlands. It was another experimental community of people trying to live simply and search for the truth. Initially, Isaac was impressed with the way Fruitlands was run. He enjoyed the intense conversations they had, especially over dinner and in the early hours of the evening. But something was missing. Individual ideas and elitist small groupings of communities would not reform the world, as he believed needed to be done. Instead, influenced by Orestes Brownson's growing insight that institutional religion was the only effective means of social reform and regeneration, Isaac finally came to the realization that Brownson was on the right track. He stayed only a few weeks at Fruitlands and then announced to the leader, Bronson Alcott,[3] that he needed to be moving on. After returning to New York, he wrote to Brownson expressing his conviction that the Spirit could not act in a vacuum but needed a medium, and conversely, humans could not do this work on their own. He wanted to work to bring into being the kingdom of God on earth, but he knew it could not be just a personal endeavor. It had to come about in the context of something larger. "The church," he said, "is the only institution which has for its object the bettering of men's souls."

Therefore Hecker questioned, Which among the different denominations would best fulfill this purpose?

---

3. Bronson Alcott (1799–1888) was an educator, philosopher, reformer, abolitionist, and advocate for women's rights. One of his daughters was Louisa May Alcott, author of *Little Women*.

5

JOURNEY TOWARD THE CATHOLIC CHURCH

I feel very cheerful & at ease in perfect peace since I have consented to join the Catholic Church. Never have I felt the quietness the immovableness and the permanent rest that I now feel. It is inexpressible. I feel that essential and interior permanence which nothing exterior can disturb and that no act that it calls upon me to perform will in the least cause me to be moved by it. It is with perfect ease and gracefulness that I never dreamed of that I will unite with the Church. It will not change but fix my life.

—*Diary*, June 13, 1844

In 1843, Isaac tried to formulate his ideas on meaning in his life, reflecting on how best not only to bring about personal change but also to effect reform that would bring about a better world. On October 17, he drew a triangle in his diary. The three sides of the triangle represented the major areas of his life—personal, political, and social—in which he discerned a need for change. In the middle of the triangle, he wrote the words *religion*, *church*, and *unity*.

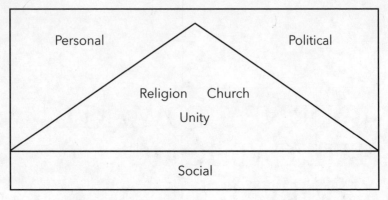

He knew that reform would come, but it would not be by individuals trying to do something on their own or in small groups. Rather, he realized, the reform that was needed in the world would be brought about by individuals becoming part of something much larger. He had a notion that organized church could provide the necessary unity and moral direction.

And so after an absence of nine months, Isaac returned home, still with no decision about what he would do with his life. He helped out his brothers at the bakery, but he also spent quite a bit of his time reading and reflecting on what direction his future would take.

More and more, Isaac was coming to believe that institutional church would be more effective than either personal or even politically oriented social action in bringing about the reforms he perceived were needed. He kept in touch with Orestes Brownson, to whom he wrote,

> The necessity for a medium through which the Spirit can act, that man as man can be no reformer, and that the church is the only institution which has for its object the bettering of men's souls, are clear and important to me.

At one point, Isaac had some conversations with his brother John's pastor, Rev. Benjamin Haight, at All Saints Episcopal Church, but the conversations did not answer any of his questions satisfactorily.

An entry in Isaac's diary on his twenty-fourth birthday, December 18, 1843, indicates that he still had not found what he was looking for. Once again he tried the Methodist faith of his mother, but it still left him wanting.

In 1844, Isaac came to a new juncture on his journey through life. Believing strongly that God acted through the church, he decided that he wanted to study for the ministry. The question was, should he become a Catholic priest or an Episcopal minister? While trying to resolve this question, he confided his intentions to Brownson. Brownson encouraged him and recommended that, in the meantime, he prepare by studying Greek and Latin. And so Isaac decided to move to Concord, Massachusetts, where he rented a room in the home of Henry Thoreau and his mother and studied with George Bradford, a classical scholar from Harvard.

Before the move, however, Isaac made some inquiries to help him to decide which church was the right one for him. In February of 1844, he had an interview with the prominent Episcopal minister Dr. Samuel Seabury. The conversation was warm and friendly. Seabury did not push the young man in either direction, but suggested that he look closely at the good and bad points of both churches before finally making up his mind. In the course of the conversation, Seabury subtly pointed out that he himself would feel uncomfortable about such Catholic claims as papal power and infallibility. Still, Isaac's account of the conversation written in his diary indicates that he was tending toward Rome. "I told [Seabury] that though the Church of Rome may commit errors in practice," he wrote, "they had not committed any in principle and that it was easier to prune a luxuriant tree than to revivify a tree almost exhausted of life."

JOHN HENRY NEWMAN

It is remarkable how closely Hecker's thought processes at this preconversion stage resemble those of Newman and the English converts who followed Newman to the Church of Rome. Not for nothing had he read the *Tracts for the Times*. Later, close ties between the early Paulists and some members of Newman's Oratory in Birmingham, England, would also reflect their common paths to Rome.

Isaac's interview with Bishop John Hughes of New York had a less happy outcome. Somewhat standoffish and aloof, Hughes lectured him on Catholic authority and discipline. The young seeker did not necessarily have anything against submitting to discipline, but the bishop's severe emphasis on it squelched Isaac's idea of becoming a Catholic for the time being.

And so, still without having reached a decision, he went off to Concord, where he divided his time between study and prayer. The prayer brought him such peace and joy that he began to fear that the studies would "quench the flow of life from within," as he wrote to Brownson, confiding that he was thinking of dropping the studies.

Brownson recognized a red flag when he saw one. This time the often dilatory correspondent replied immediately, urging Isaac not to give up his studies. Isaac was in danger of being led astray by a comfortable "mystical" life. Brownson pointed out, "Your cross is to resist the tendency to mysticism, to sentimental luxury which is really enfeebling your soul and preventing it from attaining to true spiritual blessedness." Then Brownson disclosed that he had made up his mind to enter the Catholic Church, and he encouraged Isaac to do the same. Eventually, suggested Brownson, he might serve as a priest in the Midwest, where there was a large German immigrant population.

Brownson's news caused Isaac to revisit his own thoughts on the Catholic Church. His mentor arranged for him to meet with the coadjutor bishop of Boston, John Fitzpatrick. Over the course of a few meetings, Bishop Fitzpatrick concluded that Isaac should be baptized a Catholic. In the process, he suggested two things: one, that he be brought into the church in New York rather than in Boston, because that was where Isaac had many friends; two, that Isaac spend some time getting acquainted with the Jesuits at the new Holy Cross College in Worcester, Massachusetts.

After spending three days with the Jesuits at Holy Cross, Isaac stopped by Brook Farm to visit his old friends who were still there, explaining to them his journey to the Catholic Church. He recounted some of his struggles, as a youth, trying to find meaning in his daily life. He talked at length about his relationship with God, how he felt called to spend his life in service to God. His friends encouraged him to continue on his quest to find peace and meaning in his life. They even suggested that someday he might write a book about his searching.

Upon returning to New York, Isaac visited the coadjutor bishop, John McCloskey, to whom Bishop Fitzpatrick had given him a letter of introduction. Bishop McCloskey was impressed by the potential convert's knowledge of Catholic teaching. On August 2, 1844, after a few weeks of instruction, Bishop McCloskey baptized Isaac Hecker at Old St. Patrick's Cathedral. "The Catholic Church," wrote Isaac, "is my star, which will lead me to my life, my destiny, my purpose."

Bishop McCloskey continued to be Isaac's spiritual director. He encouraged him to continue his Greek and Latin studies. Here was a potential candidate for the priesthood, he thought, but he did not want to put any pressure on the young man. While deciding what course of action to take, Isaac returned to the family business and also took courses at the Cornelius Academy. He wasn't quite sure how to fit in there, since the other young men were Protestant. When his studies ended, he concluded that Protestantism had not the resources to improve the world; his experiences, he wrote, gave him an insight into Protestantism's "want of deep spirituality, its superficiality and its inevitable tendency to no religion."

Isaac was convinced, as was Bishop McCloskey, that God would eventually reveal to him the course he was to take. In the meantime, he considered various options, including the diocesan priesthood and the well-known religious orders. These included the Redemptorists, whose Church of the Holy Redeemer in Lower Manhattan Isaac came to visit frequently. From there came the answer that Isaac had spent so long seeking. He had come to know the church's pastor, Fr. Gabriel Rumpler. One day Fr. Rumpler introduced him to two young converts, Clarence Walworth and James McMaster, who had decided to join the Redemptorist priesthood and were soon to sail to Belgium to the order's novitiate.

Isaac's mind was made up. He would sail with them on that ship to study to be a Redemptorist priest.

6

JOINING THE REDEMPTORISTS

The Catholic faith rests upon three elementary facts—
the competency of human reason, the infallibility of the
Church, the veracity of God. He who undermines...one
of these three positions destroys the Catholic faith.

—Fr. Hecker, *The Church and the Age*, 1887

The ship to Europe was leaving the next day. Isaac asked if he could go with Clarence Walworth and James McMaster, because he, too, wanted to join the novitiate. Fr. Rumpler explained that Isaac would have to get permission from the provincial, who was at that time in Baltimore.

Isaac traveled all night and arrived at the Redemptorist foundation in Baltimore at about four o'clock in the morning. He met with Fr. de Held, the provincial, explained to him why he was there, and handed him a number of letters of recommendation from the Redemptorists in New York. Fr. de Held read the letters and conducted an impromptu interview. When asked why he wanted to be a Redemptorist, Isaac said he wanted to gain his own sanctification and lead others to God.

After permission was given and the proper papers signed, Isaac rushed back to New York to join Walworth and McMaster.

Isaac's brother George, having had a feeling earlier that day that Isaac would get the permission to go, packed his suitcase and met him at the dock so that Isaac would not miss the ship, which was ready to take leave for England. On the voyage, Isaac got to know the two companions who would be part of his novitiate class once they arrived at St. Trond. From the London dock, they proceeded to Antwerp and then on to the novitiate.

After they spent about three weeks getting settled in and used to the novitiate schedule, Isaac and his classmates were given the Redemptorist habit to wear. The habit was a floor-length outer garment made of black cloth. It had a white collar attached to it that could be taken off easily and washed, and a cincture that was used around the waist to keep the habit closed in the front. A large rosary hung from the cincture off to the side.

The language spoken at the novitiate was French. The novices studied the community's constitution and rules and lived according to the schedule given them. They learned obedience to the rules and schedule, as well as obedience to whatever their superiors told them to do. It was a test for living in community under a specific set of rules and way of life.

Their day was divided up into periods of time in which certain tasks were to be accomplished. Each period of time was started by the ringing of a bell. The daily schedule ran as follows:

4:30	Rise
5:00	Meditation and prayer
5:30	Mass and thanksgiving and reading of the rule
7:30	Breakfast and manual labor
8:30	Rosary, spiritual reading, and Stations of the Cross
10:45	Reading and meditation

12:00	Dinner while listening to spiritual reading
1:30	Prayers
2:00	Free time
2:45	Visit to the Blessed Sacrament
3:00	Reading of the lives of saints
4:00	Recitation of the Divine Office
5:15	Recreation
6:00	Memorization of the constitution of the community
7:00	Meditation
7:30	Supper
8:15	Prayers
9:00	Lights out

Thursdays and principal feasts were recreational.

The novice director, Fr. Othman, was a bit suspicious of Isaac because he was much more spiritual than the normal person who was entering the novitiate for the first time. Fr. Othman kept a close watch over him to see if he might be faking his sincerity. Often, when the others went on the day-off walk, Fr. Othman would make Isaac stay behind and do some manual labor, such as washing the hall floors. This was to test his ability to obey, and to assure the novice master that Isaac had sufficient humility. After a few months of this severe testing, Fr. Othman was convinced that Isaac was a worthy candidate. He relaxed his strictness.

Isaac and his classmates made their final profession on the feast day of St. Teresa of Avila, October 15. McMaster, one of the Americans who came with Isaac from America, was not with this group. The novice director had asked McMaster to leave because he felt that he did not have a vocation to be a Redemptorist.

WITTEM CONVENT

Following their novitiate, Isaac Hecker and his classmates continued study-ing for the priesthood at the Redemptorist seminary in Wittem Limbourg in the Netherlands.

The novices were then sent to the seminary at Wittem Limbourg to continue their studies for the priesthood. Isaac studied philosophy. Walworth studied theology. Since they were studying different courses, the two Americans hardly ever saw each other on any given day.

Each seminarian had different chores to perform. Some had to wash floors; others worked in the repair shop. Some were assigned to the laundry room; a few were chosen as sacristans. Others became infirmarians. Since he was a good baker, one of Isaac's house jobs was to bake the bread. He also helped bring the wood in for the ovens.

Although everyone liked Isaac and wanted him to be a Redemp-torist, his studies were not going too well. Even so, the superiors allowed him to receive the tonsure[1] at the end of his first year of studies.

At the beginning of Isaac's second year in the seminary, he was made infirmarian and so spent the year caring for the sick in his

---

1. Tonsure refers to the shaving of the top of the head so that the rest of one's hair looked as if it were forming a crown. A rite of passage for those to be ordained a priest, tonsure was the sign that a person was no longer a layperson but a cleric.

community. He did not take formal classes that year, but he did continue to read theological books. One of his favorite books at the time was *Spiritual Doctrine* by Louis Lallemant, SJ. Although before he entered the seminary there were a number of entries in his diary on his thoughts concerning the Holy Spirit, it seems that Isaac learned a great deal from Lallemant's book about the inner workings of the Holy Spirit. As a result, he regularly sought the Holy Spirit's guidance in all that he did. This book may have been the inspiration for the spirituality Isaac developed regarding the Holy Spirit in later life.

It is interesting that his devotion to the Holy Spirit began earlier in his life, as entries in his diary indicate. On June 7, 1844, he wrote, "It is not by secluding from the world that we are strengthened in practical virtue. It is a sin to divert our attention to reading when God would fill our hearts with the fullness of the Holy Ghost." On July 5 of that year, he wrote his thoughts and prayed:

> We should encourage all that gives us an impulse heavenward and deny all that tends to draw us down more in the body-sense and time. Man alas is weak powerless and unable to perform any good deed to raise himself to God to serve heaven without the free gift of the blessed grace of God the Holy Spirit.
>
> We all fail to act up to the divine grace which is given us. Oh Lord forgive me my manifold transgressions and empower me to be more and more obedient to Thy Holy Spirit. It is the desire of inward Man to follow thy Spirit.

As an adult, Isaac relied heavily on the presence of the Holy Spirit that he felt in his life. He recognized that the Holy Spirit, God's Spirit, held things together, inspired people's thinking, and directed people's lives.

In August of 1848, Clarence Walworth was ordained a priest and was sent to England to work. Isaac was also sent to England to further his studies. Again, Isaac and studies were not a good mix. Unable to concentrate sufficiently, he did not do well in the classroom. The superior did not know what to do. Hecker's confessor, a Redemptorist priest named Fr. Buggenoms, said he would take Isaac under his wing and guarantee that he would be able to pass the test for priesthood, if the superior allowed him to undertake a special project.

With that assurance from Fr. Buggenoms, Fr. de Held, the superior, came to respect Isaac and actually befriended him. At Fr. de Held's request, Isaac wrote a rather lengthy paper clarifying his feelings and thoughts on a number of important topics, including the Real Presence in the Eucharist; doing God's will; personal self-discipline; selfless love of God; communion with some of the saints; and being in the presence of the Lord.

At the end of the year, Isaac passed the test given to qualify for priesthood, and on October 23, 1849, he was ordained a priest on the community's feast of the Most Holy Redeemer.

FROM ENGLAND TO AMERICA

In 1850, Fr. Bernard Hafkenscheid became provincial in the United States and asked to have Fathers Walworth and Hecker assigned there.

The two left for New York in January 1851. On March 19, the feast day of St. Joseph, they arrived in New York harbor. Isaac was greeted by his family, and later that day he went to his new home, the Redemptorist foundation on Third Street.

In April, Isaac, though a little nervous about it, took part in his first mission, which was held at St. Joseph's Church on Washington Place in New York City.

AUGUSTINE HEWIT

One of the original band of Paulists, Fr. Augustine Hewit was the son of a prominent Congregationalist minister from Connecticut. After a brief period as an Episcopalian, he became one of many who followed John Henry Newman into the Catholic Church. Fr. Hewit succeeded Isaac Hecker as Superior General of the Paulists.

Another American convert joined this band of missionaries with Isaac. His name was Fr. Augustine Hewit. Fr. Hewit was a diocesan priest before joining the Redemptorists. Before that he had been an Episcopalian and, originally, a Calvinist. Isaac started out on the mission band giving some of the instructions, but quickly graduated to giving some of the main sermons. He held people's attention. He had come to know and understand the American mind.

The small band of missionaries conducted a number of missions, staying on the road for weeks. They preached in Loretto, Pennsylvania; Johnstown, Ohio; Youngstown, Ohio; Mount St. Mary's in Emmitsburg, Maryland; St. Peter's in New York City; and even Old St. Patrick's Cathedral. They went on to Detroit, Michigan; Wheeling, West Virginia; Cincinnati, Ohio; Louisville, Kentucky; Albany, New York; Richmond, Virginia; Baltimore, Maryland; and New Orleans, Louisiana. Each time they not only preached their missions to Catholics, but also directed some of their words toward any Protestants who may have been in the audience.

GEORGE DESHON

Another member of the original band of Paulists, Fr. George Deshon graduated second in his class from the U.S. Military Academy, where he was a classmate and roommate of Ulysses S. Grant. The engineering training he received at West Point proved useful later on when, as a Paulist, he superintended the building of the Church of St. Paul the Apostle in New York. Fr. Deshon became the third Superior General of the Paulists.

Early in 1856, Fr. Walworth became the superior. In that same year, Fr. George Deshon, who had been a roommate of Ulysses S. Grant while at West Point, joined their mission band. Fr. Deshon had been a convert to Catholicism.

Shortly before this, Francis Baker, a convert, joined the Redemptorists. Baker was ordained in November of 1856 and was assigned to the mission band.

As a result of Isaac's popularity on the mission band, especially with the Protestants to whom he spoke, Isaac had an idea for a book. He wanted to write about his journey to becoming a Catholic and explain how he found the teachings of the Catholic Church to express the ideas and ideals that he had been searching and longing for as a young adult. Nothing like this had yet been written in the United States by an American for the Americans who were searching. Many of his friends and associates encouraged him to write it. In 1855, Hecker's book, *Questions of the Soul*, was published. It turned Isaac Hecker from an almost unknown (but hardworking) priest to a nationally known spokesperson for the Catholic Church. *Questions of the Soul* perfectly captured the mindset of Hecker's American contemporaries: that sense of excitement of being free from the past and open to the future, a truly "New World" sense that was also expressed so well in the art and literature of the age. He avoided the usual Catholic approach of refuting Protestant errors and using history to prove the validity of the Catholic Church. Instead, he established the sense of the times and the claim that each person's task is "to find his destiny, or to make one."

> "Who am I"? "Whence did I come"? "Whither do I tend"? "Who is God"? "What are my relations to God? To man? To the world around me"? "Have I a destiny? A work to do? What is it? And where? Or is all ruled by fate? Or left to what men called chance"?

It is not difficult to see that he was speaking from his own experience, and he had always believed that his experience was by no means unique. Each person had a destiny; each person had a work to do. He extracted from his own life journey to describe what he believed to be common to humankind and especially to the American at this point in time. The human individual needed God, and the human individual needed the church to provide "unerring and divine guidance" to which he or she could submit. Hecker then went on to demonstrate Protestantism's inadequacy to the task. Rome, on the other hand, spoke with divine, not human authority, offering guidance and the sacraments, especially penance and the Eucharist. Catholicism answered the questions to which each soul must come to terms. The last chapter ends,

> America presents to the mind, at the present epoch, one of the most interesting questions, and one too, of the greatest moment for the future destiny of man; the question, Whether the Catholic Church will succeed in Christianizing the American people as she has Christianized all European nations, so that the Cross of Christ will accompany the stars and stripes in our future?
>
> We say that this question is fraught with great interest for the future of humanity. Our people are young, fresh, and filled with the idea of great enterprises; the people who, of all others, if once Catholic, can give a new, noble, and glorious realization to Christianity; a development which will go even beyond the past in achievements of zeal, in the abundance of saints, as well as in art, science, and material greatness. The Catholic Church alone is able to give unity to a people, composed of such conflicting elements as ours, and to form them into a great nation.

The book became quite popular and went through a number of editions. The preface to the sixth edition, printed in 1868, states,

The age is out of joint. Men run to and fro to find the truth. The future lies hid in obscurity and thick darkness. The wide world seems afloat. The question, Has man a destiny, and what is it? agitates the souls of all men. It would seem that God had never made known to man his destiny, or that man had missed the way that leads to it. Who will bring the light of truth once more to dawn upon the soul? Truth that will give man life, energy, and purpose worthy of his noble and Godlike capacities? One thing we can truly say of the following sheets; they are not idle speculations. Our heart is in them, and our life's results. That they may be a means to answer life's problem to earnest souls, is our only ambition. With this, knowing that truth is never spoken in vain, we send them forth.

The success of *Questions of the Soul* motivated Hecker to follow with a second book. Titled *Aspirations of Nature*, it was published in 1857. By this time, having amassed considerable experience in preaching missions around the country, he felt confident that he had gained sufficient insight into the pulse of his countrymen to be able to speak to their deepest needs and to evangelize them. Americans were, he saw, open to a transcendent dimension in life but lacked direction. The time was ripe for Catholicism:

The new world promises a new civilization. And in this unfettered civilization, true Religion will find a reception it has in vain looked for elsewhere and a development of unprecedented glory. For religion is never so attractive and beautiful as when connected with intelligence and free conviction.

He made the case for Catholicism by examining Protestantism and finding it wanting, largely because of the implications of its theory of human depravity. Catholicism was unfettered by such a belief, he observed; it had an optimistic view of human reason, free will, and human dignity. The human being had a natural aspiration toward God, and the Catholic Church and its teachings were there to direct and help fulfill this aspiration. The book concluded,

> America! You who look for Religion agreeing with your intelligence, commensurate with all the wants of your nature, and which presents a destiny worthy of your highest efforts, investigate the claims of the Catholic Religion, and exercise your freedom by paying a loyal homage to its Divine Truth.

Aspirations of Nature was much more controversial than *Questions of the Soul* and did not enjoy such a favorable reception. It was almost as if Isaac had been writing in a vacuum, unaware of the Know Nothing movement, which fanned anti-Catholicism to new life and cast doubt on Catholics' ability to be patriotic Americans. Nonetheless, the two books, coming so closely together, helped him to achieve recognition as a leader of the Catholic Church in America.

AN ENGLISH-SPEAKING HOUSE FOR THE GERMAN-SPEAKING REDEMPTORISTS

In March 1856, Hecker stayed after the mission that his little band had been giving in Norfolk, Virginia, and gave three lectures to Protestants. In this way he took the initiative to fulfill the wishes of Fr. Ruland, the provincial of the New York Redemptorists, for outreach to non-Catholics.

The work of the mission band was thriving. Their reputation was spreading around the country and they were in constant demand. Because of this work, which was done primarily in English, a number of bishops had the idea of asking the Redemptorist Superior General in Rome to start an English-speaking foundation in the United States. Until then, all the foundations spoke German and ministered to the German-speaking immigrants that were settling in the United States. Both Bishop Bayley of Newark and Bishop Hughes of New York petitioned the Redemptorist authorities in Rome with this idea. In July of 1857, the answer came back: No!

Later that month, Fr. Clarence Walworth wrote a letter to the Superior General stating his belief that it was a good idea to utilize the English-speaking Redemptorists in an endeavor that was already producing excellent results. Although Fr. Walworth felt that the English-speaking house should be in New York, he did not believe he had the power or the right to send an emissary to Fr. Mauron, the Superior General in Rome, to propose this idea.

The Redemptorist constitutions allowed a member to go to Rome and speak to the Superior General if there was a serious reason to do so. However, due to an incident in which a priest had traveled at great expense to see the Superior General on matters that were not of any particular importance, the Superior General had sent out a letter forbidding anyone to travel to Rome to speak to him. In this way he wanted to prevent frivolous matters from being brought to him, often at great expense to the community. As good Americans, Frs. Hecker, Hewit, Walworth, Baker, and Deshon regarded the community's constitution as a higher authority than the Superior General. They decided to take the risk, and they sent Hecker to Rome with their request. They reasoned that the constitution was on their side, so there should be no problem with one of their members following the spirit and the letter of the constitution.

TROUBLES IN ROME

George Hecker bought Isaac's boat ticket for the trip to Rome. Isaac left on August 5, 1857, and arrived in Rome three weeks later. He brought with him a letter from the Archbishop of New York, a letter of good standing in the community from Isaac's local superior Fr. Ruland, a letter from Bishop Bayley of Newark, and a variety of other letters from Redemptorists and people of note whose names would be easily recognizable by the hierarchy in Rome. All the letters spoke highly of Fr. Hecker and of the idea of starting an English-speaking Redemptorist foundation in the United States. Hecker planned to present these letters to the Superior General to show that the idea did not simply originate with a small band of American-born Redemptorists.

When Hecker arrived at the Redemptorist headquarters, things did not go well. Although he was cordially greeted, he was told that the Superior General was in meetings with his council, and that Isaac would be seen in a few days. Then, when Isaac came at the appointed time for his meeting, he was told that he would not been seen or heard; in fact, since he had come without the proper permission, the only recourse the Superior General and his council had was to dismiss him from the community for his act of disobedience.

Needless to say, Isaac was stunned. He left the room and went immediately to the chapel to pray and collect himself. After a short while, he went back in to the room where the Superior General and his council were meeting. On his knees, he begged to be heard. His pleas were denied.

Outside, walking down the street, Isaac did not know what

he was going to do. He could not believe how unfairly he had been treated. Surely, there must be some recourse! He looked around and found a place to stay. He wrote a letter home to the four Americans who were anxiously waiting for some word from him, and explained what had happened. He said he would try to get a proper hearing and be reinstated. He wrote to his brother George as well, informing him of what had happened.

CARDINAL BARNABÒ

After Isaac Hecker's summary expulsion from the Redemptorists, Cardinal Alessandro Barnabò arranged for an interview between Hecker and Pope Pius IX, who reversed the order of expulsion and later approved the plan to create a new, American congregation of priests.

With great patience and over time, Isaac was able to make friends with two high-ranking officials at the Vatican. Cardinal Alessandro Barnabò was Prefect of Propaganda Fide, the Vatican congregation that oversaw missionary activity, and Archbishop Bedini was its Secretary. Both were important allies, not only because they were high-ranking officials but also because they were on very friendly terms with the pope. They found Isaac very affable and liked his new ideas for the conversion of America. With their help, negotiations, and behind-the-scenes conversations, Isaac was hopeful that some good would come from the predicament in which he found himself.

As news of Hecker's dismissal reached the United States, he continued to receive letters of support from home. Many of these letters came from bishops in whose dioceses Isaac had given missions and retreats. During his time in Rome, he received additional letters of support from Bishop Kenrick of Baltimore, Maryland; Bishop Barry of Savannah, Georgia; Bishop Purcell of Cincinnati, Ohio; Bishop Lynch of Charleston, South Carolina; Bishop Goesbriand of Burlington, Vermont; and Bishop Spalding of Louisville, Kentucky. He secured the help of friends in Rome too: Msgr. Kirby from the Irish College and Dr. B. Smith, a noted Benedictine.

To help bolster his image while he was in Rome, Hecker wrote two articles for *Civiltà Cattolica*, a Jesuit journal read by the Pope. The first described the growth enjoyed by Catholicism in the United States and pointed out how ripe the time was for the evangelization of those who were not yet Catholics but were searching for the truth in their lives. In his second article, he wrote of God's hand in the life and times of Americans, preparing them for conversion. The times were ripe and the American constitution gave religious denominations a free hand in persuading people to join them. Americans were looking for a positive religion to meet all their hungers for the real truth. Isaac Hecker was there ready and willing to fill that void.

After Isaac had published his ideas for the conversion of the people of the United States, he had the opportunity to speak personally with Pope Pius IX. He, too, was impressed with Isaac's ideas for the conversion of America. It was a delicate situation, however. The other four American Redemptorists had decided to follow Isaac in either forming an English-speaking community in the United States or in forming their own religious community, if need be. The Pope was interested in Isaac and what his little band of American priests could do to make Catholicism a major force in America, but he also knew that he could not upset the balance of power in the Redemptorists by completely siding with Isaac's group. It was finally decided that the Pope would dispense the five Americans from their vows with the Redemptorists and grant them permission to form a new community dedicated to the conversion of America. On March 6, 1858, seven months after Isaac arrived in Rome, Pope Pius IX officially gave Isaac Hecker his blessing to begin a new community in the United States. They were to be a missionary society to the United States, for the people of the United States, by priests primarily from the United States. The Pope expected them to work under the direction of the U.S. bishops. Their primary work was to save souls.

Isaac immediately wrote back to the United States with the wonderful news. The four priests were relieved that their dilemma was solved. He spent the next few days preparing to leave for home, but first he had to thank the many friends who helped him tremendously during his exile time in Rome.

On March 16, Isaac met with Pope Pius IX and personally thanked him for his decision and promised he would do all in his power, as soon as he could, to get the job of converting America done. The pope gave Isaac his blessing, a blessing for his new community and for the work they were about to begin.

The last thing he did before he was free to leave for home was to visit the Superior General who had dismissed him from the Redemptorist community. It was a cordial meeting. Both hoped there would be no hard feelings about what had happened. Isaac let the Superior General know that he would continue to be in his prayers.

Isaac could now go home with a clear conscience and, with renewed vigor, start his new venture to convert America.

7

A NEW RELIGIOUS COMMUNITY

The Paulists

The true Paulist is a religious entirely depending on God
for his spiritual life, living in community, and labors
above all to supply the most pressing needs of Church
and humanity of his day.

—Fr. Hecker, *The Paulist Vocation*

When the four priests back home received their letter officially
dispensing them from their commitments with the Redemptorists,
they started making plans to find a new place to live. Isaac's brother
George had a spacious home, and he let them stay with him and
his family.

During the first few months of their being a new community, Fr. Baker had the opportunity to go back to being a diocesan
priest in Baltimore, but he chose to stay. Fr. Walworth, however,
did not agree with the way the community was being formed, and
so he returned to Albany, New York, to be a diocesan priest. Isaac
Hecker was elected the first superior. To ensure proper functioning

of the new community, one of their first tasks was to compose a set of rules that they would all agree to live by. They submitted their Rule[1] to Archbishop Hughes of the Archdiocese of New York on July 7, 1858. In the Rule they gave their community the official name of the Missionary Society of St. Paul the Apostle, a name they chose because, just as St. Paul was a missionary who spread the good news to those wanting true meaning in their lives two thousand years earlier, so, too, was this new community of men dedicated to spreading the good news as missionaries to North America. They became known as the Paulist Fathers.

THE FOUR PAULIST FOUNDERS

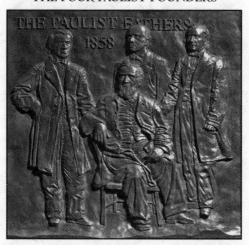

The Paulist Fathers have always found unique, individual ways to carry out their mission. This sculpture by contemporary artist Fr. Frank Sabatté, CSP, depicts the four founders of the Paulists, Frs. George Deshon, Francis Baker, Augustine Hewit, and (seated) Isaac Hecker.

---

1. The rule of a religious order consists of the guidelines to which the members agree to abide. The rule facilitates the smooth functioning of the organization and helps to ensure growth in the spiritual life and the living of the charism of the order.

Personal perfection and zeal for souls was the basis of the Paulist Rule. As good Americans, individuality was a hallmark of their commitment to one another. Hecker once said he would rather suffer from the excesses of liberty than from the arbitrary actions of tyranny. The central moving force of the community would be the guidance of the Holy Spirit.

ST. PAUL THE APOSTLE CHURCH

The thinly populated area of Manhattan around Fifty-Ninth Street and Ninth Avenue became the Paulist's first parish. This photograph shows St. Paul the Apostle Church and, in front of it, the original Paulist residence.

Shortly after the Paulists became an official community, Archbishop Hughes offered them a recently created parish on the West Side of Manhattan near Central Park. The Paulists found this a good location for their first church and foundation. The property, located between Fifty-Ninth and Sixtieth Streets west of Ninth Avenue, was pretty far out of the city center but only a few blocks west of Central Park. They lived in a rented house on Sixtieth Street, near Broadway, until a new building was completed and ready to be occupied.

Fr. Hecker was very involved in shaping his new religious community. He was interested in making sure he had an adequate house for his new community to live in and was equally concerned that the parish building be sufficient to help develop the prayer life of his parishioners.

GEORGE HECKER

Isaac remained close to his brother George throughout their lives, and it was George's business acumen, and the financial rewards reaped through it, that provided a steady support to Isaac's spiritual ventures. George died only a few months before Isaac.

As often as he was able, Isaac kept in contact with his family, who still lived on the lower east side of Manhattan. He and his brother George were particularly close. He had always hoped and prayed that all the members of his family would become Catholics. He was very close to his mother and prayed especially hard for her conversion. In 1858, however, Caroline Hecker died at the age of eighty-two. Isaac was glad that he was able to be near her at the end of her life. She had been a good mother and had sowed the seeds of faith in him as a child. Isaac felt blessed to have had her in his life as long as he had.

In the latter part of 1859, Fr. Robert Tillotson, a convert and an American who had joined Newman's Oratory[2] in England, joined the Paulists. Father Alfred Young, from the diocese of Newark, joined them soon after. Fr. Walworth rejoined them (for a while).

In 1861, Hecker started to print an annual collection of sermons preached by the Fathers during the previous year. These *Paulist Sermons*, as they were called, were very popular and sold well. Isaac had always been impressed with the spoken word, such as lectures and homilies. Now he was beginning to branch out into the written word through books, magazines, and even pamphlets.

Things ran pretty smoothly for a few years. There were enough Paulists not only to run the parish of St. Paul the Apostle at Fifty-Ninth Street, but also to keep up a pretty good pace of running missions throughout the United States and even in Canada. In April of 1865, however, Fr. Baker died, leaving the Paulists without enough priests both to run the parish and to keep the missions going. They suspended the missions until new members were of sufficient number to resume them.

THE LAUNCH OF *THE CATHOLIC WORLD* AND THE PAULIST PRESS

In 1865, Isaac started a magazine called *The Catholic World*. He wanted the magazine to be of high quality and to explain the Catholic religion in language easily understandable to most people.

---

2. The Congregation of the Oratory is a religious congregation of priests founded by St. Philip Neri (1515–95). John Henry Newman, who became an Oratorian priest after his conversion, founded the Birmingham Oratory.

It discussed religious matters of current interest, such as matters historical, fictional, and poetical, and a variety of social problems of the day. Of course, his brother George helped underwrite the new publication.

In 1866, encouraged by the popularity of his magazine, Isaac started the Catholic Publication Society, later to be called Paulist Press. He began by publishing tracts and pamphlets to tell, in simple words, the facts about the Catholic faith. Initially the idea was that church groups around the country would buy the pamphlets at cost and then distribute them for free.

One of the first tracts ended with an earnest plea for the non-Catholic to take a closer look into the Catholic Church:

> Reader, would you be honest and do no injustice? Then examine the doctrines of the Catholic Church. Read the works of Catholics. See both sides. Examine and be fair, for Americans love fair play.

THE COUNCIL OF BALTIMORE

In 1866, after the close of the Civil War, the Second Plenary Council of Baltimore[3] was convened. Addressing the Bishops of America, Isaac Hecker spoke of the marvelous future for the melding of America and the Catholic Church:

> Nowhere is there a promise of a brighter future for the Church than in our own country. Here, thanks to our

---

3. Between 1852 and 1884, the Catholic bishops in the United States held three Plenary Councils, or national meetings, in Baltimore, Maryland. During this time all of the Catholic dioceses in the United States formed one ecclesiastical province under the Archbishop of Baltimore. Archbishop Martin John Spalding presided over the Second Plenary Council, which was held between October 7 and 21, 1866.

American Constitution, the Church is free to do her divine work. Here, she finds a civilization in harmony with her divine teachings. Here, Christianity is promised a reception from an intelligent and free people, that she will give forth a development of unprecedented glory. For religion is never so beautiful as when in connection with knowledge and freedom.

Let us, therefore, arise and open our eyes to the bright future that is before us! Let us labor with a lively faith, a firm hope, and a charity that knows no bounds, by every good work and good example, for the reign of God's kingdom upon earth.[4]

At Isaac's suggestion, the bishops passed legislation to pay for the tracts. However, the money was not forthcoming because other pressing matters took precedence once the bishops returned to their home dioceses. They had, among other things, schools and churches to build.

Of course, Isaac's beloved brother George continued to open his "deep pockets" whenever necessity required it. George always admired the work Isaac was doing. He wanted to be supportive of Isaac, not only with brotherly love but also from the bounty he had amassed running the successful Hecker Flour Company. He financed Isaac's publication endeavors.

PARTICIPANT AT VATICAN I

In 1869, the Pope summoned the ecumenical council that came to be called Vatican Council I. The Council was convoked on

---

4. Paulist Archives from Hecker's talk called *Future Triumph of the Church*, October 1866.

December 8, 1869. Hecker went as a proxy for Bishop Rosecrans of Columbus, Ohio, who was too sick to go himself; but he was unable to get into the meetings. There were so many bishops, there was no room for proxies. To help Isaac out of his predicament, the Archbishop of Baltimore, Martin John Spalding, made him his personal theologian. As a result, Isaac got all the material that was handed out at the Council to be read.

While in Rome, Fr. Hecker met up with his old friend Cardinal Barnabò, who had been so helpful to him when Isaac and his friends were dismissed by the Redemptorists in 1857–58. Hecker brought him the gift of a gold knife. The Cardinal had a rule never to accept gifts from anyone, but in light of his great affection for Isaac and the work he was doing in America, the Cardinal broke his rule and kept the knife.

Isaac also spent some time looking at many different church designs. He thought that it might be useful to him when he started building his dream church, the future basilica on Fifty-Ninth Street in New York City.

Hecker had great hopes for the Vatican Council. He was positive that, by the working of the Holy Spirit, the church and the modern world would finally see eye to eye. He felt that his efforts to convert America would spread throughout the world because of the work that would be accomplished at the Council.

While in Rome, Isaac tried to influence the Council with his democratizing ideas, but the times were not ripe for these new American ways of doing things. It was, however, only twenty years later that Pope Leo XIII started to speak to the world of the problems generated by the Industrial Revolution. Leo XIII's encyclical *Rerum Novarum* upheld the rights of the working class (including the right of workers to form and join unions) and the right to own private property, and opposed communism and unrestricted capitalism. *Rerum Novarum* is considered the first official document to express Catholic Social Teaching, that is, the body of teachings that establishes basic principles of human dignity and the common good, and advocates how government and people in society should be treating one another. Thus Leo's thoughts became the forerunner of what eventually would be called Catholic Social Justice. (Isaac was a man with futuristic ideas and plans, some of which only came to fruition with John XXIII's opening of Vatican II to continue the work that Vatican I never had a chance to address.)

On his way home from the Council, before it was finished, Isaac traveled to a number of cities in Italy. He spent time in Assisi, one of his favorite locations in Italy. He prayed and offered Mass at St. Francis's tomb. It was on this trip that he formulated some of his ideas to reconvert Europe by starting foundations in some of the major capitals of Europe.

The Council concluded after Hecker arrived home. One of the major pronouncements that came from the Council was a decree of papal infallibility, which states that when a pope speaks on matters of doctrine and morals, he cannot make an error in his judgment. When he heard about this, Isaac quipped that now the church could get on with other important matters.

In October 1870 Isaac attempted to reach out to young people by starting a publication for them called *The Young Catholic*. His sister-in-law Josephine, George's wife, produced the magazine. Though a good idea, it was short-lived. The publication ended in the mid-1870s.

8

HECKER'S LATER DAYS

All our difficulties are favors from God; we see them on the wrong side, and speak as the block of marble would while being chiseled by the sculptor. When God purifies the soul, it cries out just like little children do when their faces are washed.

—*The Paulist Vocation*

Beginning in 1871, Hecker was frequently beset with illness. Leaving the community in the capable hands of Fr. Hewit, he followed his doctor's suggestion and went south for the winter. In the summer of 1872, however, still not feeling well, he decided to go to Europe to take some of the cures at the different medicinal spas that had cropped up around the continent. The following year, not yet recovered, he traveled to Switzerland, accompanied by Fr. Deshon, but found no lasting relief there either. Eventually he headed to Egypt, where he spent four months traveling up and down the Nile River. Finally, he found some relief and actually started to relax a bit.

After leaving Egypt, he returned to Europe and was in Lyons, France, when he learned of his brother John's death. He felt badly that he was so far away and not able to be with his family to help console them.

When Isaac finally returned to the United States in October 1875, he still was not feeling strong enough to start work again at Fifty-Ninth Street, and so he moved in with his brother George in New Jersey. He stayed with George for four years, all the while maintaining frequent contact with the Fathers at Fifty-Ninth Street. Toward the end of his time at George's house, Caroline Hecker, Isaac's niece, a professional artist, painted a portrait of him. It was a painting many people admired over the years. Although a number of her paintings are in the art museum in San Diego, California, the portrait of her uncle got lost and its whereabouts are a mystery to this day.

RETURN TO THE COMMUNITY

At the end of the 1870s, Hecker moved permanently back to Fifty-Ninth Street. In early 1875, he had begun to write a long article on the problems and needs of the present age. He regarded it as the outline of what would eventually become a lengthier book. In the outline, he wrote extensively about the working of the Holy Spirit in the lives of people. He called the Holy Spirit a light and a guide to help people to come to an understanding of the kingdom of God, which abides in them. Eventually, some of the ideas appeared in a book he published in 1887 called *The Church and the Age*, a collection of his writings on a number of subjects that he wrote during the years between 1875 and 1887, mostly for *The Catholic World*. They were reflective articles on the workings of the Holy Spirit. He continued to see the church as Christ working in the world today and continued to dream of a unity of purpose between church and state or, perhaps more, between religion and politics. All of this, he felt, was done with and through the powerful influence of the workings of the Holy Spirit.

At the beginning of the book, Hecker states its main purpose to be

> to show that the liberty enjoyed in modern society, in so far as it is true, and the intelligence of modern society, in so far as it is guileless, are inestimable helps to the spread of Catholicity and the deepening of the interior spirit which is the best result of true religion.
>
> The office of divine external authority in religious affairs in providing a safeguard to the individual soul and assisting it to a freer and more instinctive cooperation with the Holy Spirit's interior inspirations is often treated of in this book; and the false liberty of pride and error is plainly pointed out.
>
> The main question of the hour is, How can religion be made compatible with a high degree of liberty and intelligence?

Found within the pages of this book were themes he tried to impress upon people throughout his days in ministry. They included his abiding sense of God's presence in his life and in the life of the world; his belief in equality for all, freedom for all, and the recognition of human dignity of all; his belief in the uplifting destiny of the American people; his deep devotion to the Catholic Church, and its role in the future of our society.

Isaac had grown old and tired, and unbeknownst to him, his life's work would soon come to its completion. He had faithfully done God's will in his life. He would soon meet his Maker.

ISAAC HECKER IN THE 1880S

For the last eighteen years of his life, Isaac continued his ministry to the American people while battling ever more serious illness. This photograph shows him in the 1880s.

THE END

On February 14, 1888, during the last year of Isaac's life, his brother George died. Sensing that his own end was near, Isaac resigned himself to that fact. A sense of peace came upon him as he felt the presence of the Holy Spirit engulfing him in a new way. He found solace in the fact that the Holy Spirit was, indeed, the director of his soul.

From October through December 1888, Isaac drifted in and out of a comatose state. Aware that the end was near, his Paulist community kept vigil at his bedside. After blessing those present in his room, the earnest seeker found that which all his life he sought. Four days after his sixty-ninth birthday, on December 22, 1888, Isaac Hecker died.

FR. HECKER'S TOMB (DETAIL)

This detail of the base of Fr. Hecker's tomb, located in the back of St. Paul the Apostle Church, expresses his vision of "a future for the church brighter than any past."

He was buried in Old St. Patrick's Cathedral. When the new basilica was completed at Fifty-Ninth Street, his remains were reburied in the crypt at the base of one of its towers. On the occasion of the one hundredth anniversary of the founding of the Paulists, a monumental tomb was erected in the main part of the upper church where Fr. Hecker's remains were placed.

9

THE PAULISTS TODAY

The Holy Spirit is at work among Chinese, Moslems,
and all nations, peoples and tribes, in every rational soul.
The love of God, so to speak, compels this. We may not
see or understand its secret operations, but the truth of
this is none the less true for that.

—The Paulist Vocation

Today, the Paulist Fathers continue to bring Isaac Hecker's ideals to
the North American scene by bringing the good news to people in
a language they easily understand, utilizing the most modern means
available: TV, radio, the Internet. The website www.BustedHalo.
com, designed to be of interest to young adults looking for answers
in their life, has become very popular. Paulist Press, the oldest
Catholic press in America, continues to publish high-quality books
exploring the latest trends in Catholic thinking. In addition to
parishes, the Paulist Fathers also staff Catholic campus ministry
centers at secular colleges and universities.

BAPTISMAL FONT, ST. PAUL THE APOSTLE

Water from the baptismal font at St. Paul the Apostle Church symbolizes the waters of life to which Isaac Hecker and his followers strove to bring the people to whom they preached and ministered.

In 2008, the Paulists celebrated their 150th anniversary. A national celebration, held in Washington, DC, brought together Paulists, parishioners, and associates for a three-day forum. The lectures, seminars, and keynote speakers highlighted the contributions the Paulists have made to the church but, more importantly, offered a venue in which to discuss the future ministries to which the Paulists will contribute in collaboration with the laity and with the church and bishops.

The Paulists minister in a number of cities. Below is a list of current Paulist foundations and their locations.

Berkeley, CA	Holy Spirit Parish, University of California
Los Angeles, CA	St. Paul the Apostle Catholic Community

Los Angeles, CA	University Catholic Center, UCLA
Los Angeles, CA	Paulist Productions
San Francisco, CA	Old St. Mary's Cathedral/Chinese Mission
San Francisco, CA	St. Mary's School & Chinese Catholic Center
Washington, DC	Paulist Fathers House of Mission and Studies (at St. Joseph's Seminary)
Washington, DC	Paulist Evangelization Ministries (PEM), Paulist Reconciliation Ministries
Chicago, IL	Old St. Mary's Church
Boston, MA	Paulist Center
Allendale, MI	St. Luke University Parish
Grand Rapids, MI	St. Andrew's Cathedral
Grand Rapids, MI	Catholic Information Center
Lake George, NY	St. Mary's on the Lake
New York, NY	Church of St. Paul the Apostle
New York, NY	Paulist General Office
Columbus, OH	Ohio State University, St. Thomas More Newman Center
Knoxville, TN	Immaculate Conception Church
Knoxville, TN	John XXIII University Parish, University of Tennessee
Austin, TX	St. Austin Catholic Church
Austin, TX	University Catholic Center, University of Texas
Horseshoe Bay, TX	St. Paul the Apostle Church
Rome, Italy	Church of Santa Susanna

10

DECLARING ISAAC HECKER A SAINT

During the celebration of the 150th anniversary of the Paulist Fathers, Fr. Isaac Hecker's cause for sainthood was officially opened. Because of the challenges he faced and overcame in his life, he is an inspiration for us all. We pray that soon we will be able to have the honor of calling him St. Isaac Hecker, the earnest seeker, a saint for our times.

In addition to his idea that the United States' founding documents could be a perfect meld with Catholic thinking and teaching, Hecker's spirituality and his thoughts on the workings of the Holy Spirit in our lives are good reasons not only to emulate his teaching, but also to honor him with the title "Saint for our times."

Isaac Hecker was a proponent of the working of the Holy Spirit in the lives of all people. He believed we needed to look deep within ourselves and discover the indwelling of the Spirit working in our lives. It was through the working of the Holy Spirit, he believed, that we were able, eventually, to enjoy union with God. The Holy Spirit transforms us into the children of God who we were meant to be. Hecker believed that the function of the church is to assist us in that discovery.

According to Hecker, when people embraced this indwelling of the Holy Spirit, peace, harmony, justice, and the reign of God would truly take place. All that was needed was conversion, inspired by the working of the Holy Spirit deep in the hearts and minds of all, Catholics and non-Catholics alike.

The way to activate this working of the Holy Spirit is two-fold: First, we have to overcome those things that easily distract us from union with God. We are to love only God, not the things of this life. This calls for self-discipline. Second, we must replace with virtues the things that we have purged from our life. These virtues—such as faith, hope, and love—quickly lead us to union with God. Among the virtues Isaac admired most were what he called the natural virtues of prudence, temperance, fortitude, and justice. (Although he called them the natural virtues, they are generally known as the Cardinal Virtues.)

The United States was only eighty years old when Isaac Hecker was at the peak of his missionary work. He was convinced that Catholicism would make a perfect fit for the type of democracy that was forming in the United States. Catholics believed in the inherent goodness of creation and of people. Catholics championed reason and free will. It was easy to see God's hand in the ideals of the nation and its Constitution. At that time, the United States could easily be seen as the New Promised Land. Catholicism would help form the bonds of unity in politics and in neighborhoods, promoting the good nature of people that is so necessary in making a new venture work.

Grown men like to tinker with mechanical things. They like to figure out how things work. Sometimes they end up dismantling the object in order to understand how it works. Very often the object is not put back together or, when it is reassembled, sometimes there are a few parts left over.

Not so with Isaac Hecker. When Isaac was a young boy, with the help of his grandfather, he put together a wall clock that worked for forty years. Throughout his life he was always putting people, things, and ideas together so that life would be better for those around him. He formed the Paulists to bring God's good news of salvation to the people of North America. He did this by his preaching missions, by founding the Paulist Press, by founding *The Catholic World* magazine. He did it by presenting old truths in new forms and by speaking to people of his day in language and in a manner they readily understood. He was a Catholic through and through. He was an American through and through. He tried to be a Catholic American and hoped others would follow suit. It is with good reason that Isaac Hecker merits being regarded as the most significant Catholic figure in nineteenth-century America, and deserves to be considered for sainthood.

11

THE CANONIZATION PROCESS

Fr. Michael Kerrigan, CSP

The following summary describes the steps involved in the canonical procedure for causes of beatification and canonization as set forth in the Apostolic Constitution *Divinus Perfectionis Magister*, promulgated by Pope John Paul II on January 25, 1983.

1. It is necessary to wait at least five years after the death of the candidate whose cause is to be considered.

2. The bishop of the diocese in which the candidate died is responsible for beginning the cause. A *postulator* is a church official who presents a plea for beatification or canonization of a particular candidate. The postulator acts on behalf of a promoter group that has formally requested the bishop to open an investigation into the cause of the candidate. The promoter group may be a diocese, a parish, a religious congregation, or a religious association.

3. The process begins at the diocesan level. The bishop forms a diocesan tribunal to begin consideration of the proposed candidate by investigating the candidate's life and writings for evidence

of heroic virtue (the *theological virtues* of faith, hope, and love, and the *cardinal virtues* of prudence, justice, temperance, and fortitude). Documents and information are gathered. At this stage in the process, the candidate may be given the title *Servant of God*.

4. After the diocesan investigation is completed, the documentation is forwarded to the Vatican's *Congregation for the Causes of Saints*. A panel of theologians and cardinals from this Vatican congregation evaluates the candidate's life. When sufficient information and evidence have been obtained, the congregation may recommend to the pope that he make a proclamation of the Servant of God's heroic virtue and declare the candidate *Venerable*, meaning that he or she is a role model of Catholic virtues.

5. The next step, *beatification*, requires a miracle that has resulted from prayers to the candidate and the candidate's subsequent intercession. An official church investigation is done to evaluate the legitimacy of the miracle. When a miracle has been declared authentic, the candidate is given the title *Blessed*.

6. *Canonization* requires an additional miracle, one that can be attributed to the intercession of the Blessed *after* beatification. The new miracle is evaluated by the same process used for the first miracle. Once the church confirms the authenticity of the evidence supporting the second miracle, the candidate is canonized and is given the title *Saint*.

PRINTED & ELECTRONIC RESOURCES

BOOKS BY FR. HECKER

Aspirations of Nature. New York: James B. Kirker, 1857.
The Church and the Age. New York: Office of the Catholic World, 1887.
Questions of the Soul. New York: Appleton, 1855.

BOOKS ABOUT FR. HECKER

Burton, Katherine. *Celestial Homespun: The Life of Isaac Thomas Hecker*. New York: Longmans, Green & Co., 1943.

Elliott, Walter. *The Life of Father Hecker*. New York: Columbus Press, 1891.

Farina, John. *An American Experience of God: The Spirituality of Isaac Hecker*. New York: Paulist Press, 1981.

—————, ed. *Hecker Studies: Essays on the Thought of Isaac Hecker*. Ramsey, NJ: Paulist Press, 1983.

—————, ed. *Isaac T. Hecker, The Diary: Romantic Religion in Ante-bellum America*, Sources of American Spirituality. New York: Paulist Press, 1988.

Hanley, Boniface. *Paulist Father Isaac Hecker: An American Saint*. Mahwah, NJ: Paulist Press, 2008.

Holden, Vincent. *The Yankee Paul: Isaac Thomas Hecker*. Milwaukee: Bruce Publishing Co., 1958.

McSorley, Joseph. *Father Hecker and His Friends*. New York: Paulist Press, 1972.

O'Brien, David. *Isaac Hecker: An American Catholic*. Mahwah, NJ: Paulist Press, 1992.

Sedgwick, Henry D. *Father Hecker*. Boston: Small, Maynard & Co., 1900.

WEBSITES

www.paulist.org
www.bustedhalo.com
www.paulistpress.com
www.pemdc.org
www.santasusanna.org

PRAYERS

PRAYERS AND REFLECTIONS BY FATHER HECKER[1]

O Lord, forgive me my sins and save me from all errors and lead me in the path that you would have me to go. Is there no one I can go to that may open my eyes that I may see? O Lord, direct me. And if you direct me, now give me faith in your means. I am, O Father, one of your children: you know all that I do. My heart is open to your inspection. Do not let me suffer for you are tender, compassionate, and full of love. Let me see: Open my eyes, and grant that I may hear your voice more distinctly. (Diary, 1843)

The Lord has been good to me and my heart is filled with his warm love. Blessed may you be, O God, for you have given me a taste of your sweetness. . . . You have put into my heart gratitude and thankfulness and an overflowing heart of praise. I would stand still and shout and bless God. It is God in us that believes in God.

---

1. The three prayers of Fr. Hecker are taken from his Diary of 1843; the three reflections are in *The Paulist Prayer Book* on pp. 502–3, 499, and 99, respectively. Because the intention of including the prayers was so that the reader might adopt them for personal use, the three prayers have been edited to reflect modern usage and punctuation. All other material from Fr. Hecker's writings quoted in this book is reproduced as found in the cited sources.

Without the light of God we should be in total darkness and he is the only source of light. (Diary, 1843)

Now, O Lord, I ask in Jesus' name, give unto me more and more of your loving spirit. Fill my whole being that there may not remain anything but your loving kindness. My soul is bowed down before you, O Lord. Bless and bestow unto me your gift, heavenly Father. (Diary, 1843)

God offers to come and dwell in our souls. God offers you interior peace, supernatural strength, holiness, and salvation. Now what does God ask of you in return for all this? That you will act the part of a generous friend toward him, by giving God a large share of your thoughts, words, and actions. God is the magnet in the center of your hearts. God is always drawing you toward himself. God asks that you will put no obstacle in the way of his influence upon you. If disturbing causes for the moment turn you from God, like the needle which may be shaken so as to point to the East or the South, like it he calls upon you not to rest till you have found your rest again in God. (PPB)

To love creatures aside from God is sinful. To love creation in God is lawful. To love God in creatures is perfection. The transformation from the first to the last is not accomplished without time, fidelity, and great trust; accompanied also with painful struggles. Are you ready? (PPB)

The love of God and the love of humans are one. God promises his reward not to the ignorant, or to the indolent, or to the indifferent, but to those who visit the prisoner, feed the hungry, give drink to the thirsty, clothe the naked—to the doing of good works as the evidence of the true faith. (PPB)

PRAYER FOR THE CAUSE FOR FATHER HECKER

Heavenly Father,
You called your servant Isaac Thomas Hecker
To preach the Gospel to the people of North America
And, through his teaching,
To know the peace and the power of your indwelling Spirit.

He walked in the footsteps of Saint Paul the Apostle
And, like Paul, spoke your Word with a zeal for souls
And a burning love for all who come to him in need.

Look upon us this day with compassion and hope.
Hear our prayer.
We ask that through the intercession of Father Hecker,
Your servant, you might grant us [state the request].

We ask this in the name of Jesus Christ, Your Son, Our Lord,
Who lives and reigns with You and the Holy Spirit,
One God, forever and ever. Amen.

Please report all favors to:
Office of the Cause of Father Hecker
3015 4th St. NE
Washington, DC 20017-1102
www.paulist.org/hecker

ISAAC THOMAS HECKER

PRAYER FOR PAULIST VOCATIONS

Lord, lover of us all, you spoke your Word
to the world in Jesus and began
the gathering of grace which is your Kingdom.
You called Paul to be a special ambassador of your love,
bringing your word to all nations with a zeal and a passion
that echoed your own burning love for every person.
You called Father Isaac Hecker to walk in the steps of
Paul in our North American culture: that your Word would
be spoken again, with the tools of the modern age.
We ask you to call new modern missionaries, sons of
Hecker, by the power of your Holy Spirit. May they burn with
passion to bring the Gospel to today's world, that
all may know the mystery of your irrepressible love.
May they follow the Lord Jesus with the fervor of Paul and
Hecker and carry on the mission of the Paulist community.
We pray this through Christ Jesus, our Lord,
in the power of your Spirit. Amen.

The Paulist Vocation Director in New York City can be reached at
212-757-4260.